Harnessing the Harassment of Human Fears

STUDY GUIDE

Mark L. Graham, D. Min.

WESTBOW
PRESS®
A DIVISION OF THOMAS NELSON
& ZONDERVAN

WestBow Press books may be ordered through booksellers or by contacting:

WestBow Press
A Division of Thomas Nelson & Zondervan
1663 Liberty Drive
Bloomington, IN 47403
www.westbowpress.com
844-714-3454

Interior Image Credit: William Jenkins

ISBN: 978-1-6642-7142-5 (sc)
ISBN: 978-1-6642-7141-8 (e)

Library of Congress Control Number: 2022912371

Print information available on the last page.

WestBow Press rev. date: 07/19/2022

ACKNOWLEDGEMENTS

In sincere appreciation to Reverend John Jackson, missionary, church planter, professor, and lifelong friend, currently executive director of COMPASS 28:19 Short-term Missions Ministry. Without his suggestion and encouragement, this study guide would not have materialized. Thank you, John, my beloved friend and colleague in the Gospel.

To Jeff Lyons, a true friend and fruitful witness to the effectual Gospel of our Lord Jesus Christ. Thanks, Jeff, for your labors in preparing this study guide for publication. Thanks, also, to your dear wife, Rebecca, for her involvement in making this book complete and ready to serve the King's purpose. What a pleasure, Jeff, to have you serve with me in the ministry for so many years.

God desires each of us to be a unique life message of His transforming grace. Simply copying another's labor without permission can be both plagiaristic and stereotyping. Therefore, this study guide is intended to be used in its published context and complete format unless permission is given in writing by the author at www.genesisministry.org.

PREFACE

Harnessing the Harassment of Human Fears is a book not intended for a quick, collateral read. The study guide is thus intended to assist the reader to think and apply, but primarily to meditate upon the liberating truths of God which bring lasting hope and joy. May a thoughtful and prayerful peruse of this work result in the spiritual enrichment of your life and deeper fellowship with Jesus Christ.

Mark L. Graham

CHAPTER 1

Encounters, Episodes, and the Experience of Fear

1. Fear experiences are "amazingly similar at their core, symptomatically calculated…" (p. 2). The triggers, however, may be _____, _____, and _____.

   In your own words, explain what the author is saying

   _____
   _____
   _____
   _____
   _____

2. Using the diagram on page 3, discuss <u>The Fearful Episode and Effect</u>. Be sure to read the author's description of the sketch beneath the diagram.

   _____
   _____
   _____
   _____
   _____

3. Using the overview list of common fears, choose three fears, making comparisons to the experience of each while contrasting the trigger or stimuli (p. 2).

The Fear	Diverse Triggers	Fearful Effect
A. _____	1. _____	_____
	2. _____	_____
	3. _____	_____
	4. _____	_____

4. Reflect personally upon a fear episode that you have encountered in your life. Now, using the diagram on page 3 again, describe and delineate the descent of your episode.

_____

_____

_____

_____

_____

_____

5. Go back over chapter one and list each verse given in the text. Then, write out a brief explanation of each. There are three.

First: _____

_____

_____

_____

_____

_____

_____

_____

Second: _____

_____

_____

_____

_____

_____

_____

Third: _____

_____

_____

_____

_____

_____

_____

_____

Notes

CHAPTER 2

Fictitious Myths and a Familiar Case

1. According to the author, what is the greatest myth of the "fear encounter"?

   _____

   _____

   _____

   _____

   _____

2. Why is this myth identified in the book as a "self-fulfilling prophecy"?

   _____

   _____

   _____

   _____

   _____

3. From page 9, how does avoidance give "false credibility to a lie"? Use the immediate context for your own explanation.

   _____

   _____

   _____

   _____

   _____

4. Write out the last sentence on page 9 beneath the heading: "A Familiar Case." Log this principle in your memory!

   _____

   _____

   _____

   _____

5. Together with another person, or in a group discussion, describe the lesson(s) of diagram 2, "The Faith Episode and Effect."

_____

_____

_____

_____

_____

6. In the context of the fear episode, what is meant by the statement, "the issue is never the real issue" (p. 15)?

_____

_____

_____

_____

_____

7. Using the case study of David, describe the three aspects to David's fear encounter with Goliath (pp. 13, 14).

First: _____

_____

_____

_____

_____

Second: _____

_____

_____

_____

_____

Third: _____

_____

_____

_____

_____

Recall these three elements involved in the case study under scrutiny: stimuli, assessment, and action.

8. List several insightful and imparting statements that are worth remembering and recording upon examining the David and Goliath account.

    A. _____
    B. _____
    C. _____
    D. _____
    E. _____

9. What things are good to remember about the nature of God in our battle with fear (p. 16)?

    _____
    _____
    _____
    _____
    _____

10. Highlight personal help from the endnotes of chapter 2.

    _____
    _____
    _____
    _____
    _____

Notes

CHAPTER 3

Contacts, Connections, and Counsel

1. Provide a brief summary of the four stages of fear (pp. 19-24).

First: The Intake

_____

_____

_____

_____

_____

Second: Alarm

_____

_____

_____

_____

_____

Third: The Eclipse

_____

_____

_____

_____

_____

Fourth: The Spiral

_____

_____

_____

_____

_____

2. Connect diagram three below (p. 23) to a particular bout with fright that you experienced out of your past. Personalize the elements or data from your struggle and affix them to the spiral beside their proper headings (i.e. dilemma, disconnect, despair).

Diagram 3
The Fright Cycle: The Downward Trend

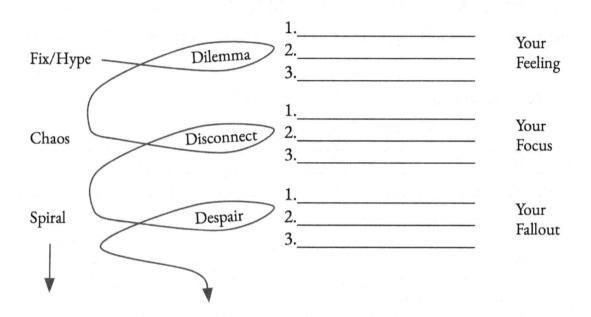

Fix/Hype — Dilemma

1._____
2._____   Your
3._____   Feeling

Chaos — Disconnect

1._____
2._____   Your
3._____   Focus

Spiral — Despair

1._____
2._____   Your
3._____   Fallout

3. Left to itself, without a check or challenge, discuss where the above spiral may have taken you. What would be the potential outcome of an uninhibited fright cycle?

_____
_____
_____
_____
_____

4. Unpack what you believe Dr. Welch is saying about contemporary medical science when he states, "behind every crooked thought there is a crooked molecule" (p. 25).

_____
_____
_____
_____
_____

5. Using the final paragraph of this chapter, relate the core lesson, primary point and fundamental overture behind biblical counseling, especially applying it to the "fear factor."

_____

_____

_____

_____

_____

6. Consult the endnotes of chapter three and briefly state the promise of the following verse.

A. 2 Timothy 1:7 (number 2)

_____

_____

_____

_____

_____

_____

B. Romans 6:14 (number 3)

_____

_____

_____

_____

_____

C. Matthew 11:28–30 (number 7)

_____

_____

_____

_____

_____

_____

Notes

CHAPTER 4

Matters of Management and Mastery

1. Interact with the author's premise that the continued battle with fear is, in essence, a natural part of faith and Christian maturity.

_____

_____

_____

_____

_____

_____

_____

2. From 1 Corinthians 10:13, what aspect of the fear encounter is relatively "out of one's control"? What aspect of it involves choice and culpability?

_____

_____

_____

_____

_____

_____

3. "The nature of temptation, then, speaks both of victim and victimizing" (p. 34). In your own words, explain and unearth the truth here in the context of 1 Corinthians 10:13.

_____

_____

_____

_____

_____

_____

4. Can you delineate a case in point when you were caught off guard by a trigger to fear? Share what choices in your thinking resulted in failure or success in your ensuing battle.

_____

_____

_____

_____

_____

_____

_____

5. Using your own case above, what lessons of faith can you learn from this valuable struggle?

_____

_____

_____

_____

_____

_____

_____

6. What impacts you most, in our discussion on fear, from St. Mark's account of the windstorm on the Sea of Galilee with Jesus and His disciples?

_____

_____

_____

_____

_____

_____

7. On page 39, the author suggests that temptation and trials are not unique. How does this knowledge help believers in their fear fight?

_____

_____

_____

_____

_____

8. How does the fact that God is faithful ensure the management of each and every irrational thought that invades our hearts and minds?

_____

_____

_____

_____

_____

_____

_____

9. Carefully read Philippians 4:9 and cite how the Apostle Paul can assure his readers of God's abiding peace. From the verse, recall his specific directives that lead to genuine peace.

_____

_____

_____

_____

_____

_____

_____

10. Discuss the use of psychotropic medication among Christians who are dealing with panic, anxiety, or irrational fears. Involve the lessons within our chapter and consider what biblical counsel you might give without criticism or censure. See Ephesians 4:15.

_____

_____

_____

_____

_____

_____

_____

Notes

CHAPTER 5

Sticks, Slingshots, and other Proven Methods

1. In your own words, what does the statement mean: "Faith does not negate effort or good sense in the employment of legitimate means to assist us in the spiritual fray" (p. 51)?

_____

_____

_____

_____

_____

_____

_____

_____

2. Explain Psalm 33:16–22 in the context of using methods and means to overcome fear.

_____

_____

_____

_____

_____

_____

_____

3. On the following page, write out short applications from the listed verses and specifically relate how these truths enable us to triumph over our fears.

   A. Psalm 44:4–8

_____

_____

_____

_____

B. Proverbs 21:31

_____

_____

_____

_____

C. 1 Samuel 17:47

_____

_____

_____

_____

4. From the discussion of "Mind Benders and Mood-Altering Meds" (p. 53, ff), respond to the following questions:

A. Why is psychotropic medication often the first thing doctors, counselors, and school officials recommend to parents who are dealing with the behavior of their children?

_____

_____

_____

_____

_____

B. How does biblical discipleship always trump a "central nervous system stimulant" as we deal with the issue of human fears?

_____

_____

_____

_____

_____

C. See chapter 3, endnote 2, and define fear, which we are to put off as Spirit-governed children of God. Additionally, read John 14:1 and observe Christ's command.

_____

_____

_____

_____

_____

D. In Christ Jesus, are you equipped to overcome the grip of fear in your life? _____ Consult the following verse as you personally think upon your answer: Colossians 2:2–10.

_____

_____

_____

_____

_____

5. Do a word study on the term "fullness" in Colossians 2:9. Since Christ dwells in the believer by the Holy Spirit, discuss, on paper, the implications of His fullness within you.

_____

_____

_____

_____

_____

_____

6. Briefly highlight the how-to plan of organizing oneself for the actual engagement with fear from pages 60–65. There are three battle-ready tasks to be done. What are these?

_____

_____

_____

_____

_____

_____

Notes

CHAPTER 6

Lateral Help for Languishing Hearts

1. Where does a true encounter with God begin (p. 77)?

   _____
   _____
   _____
   _____
   _____
   _____

2. How can even a "religious experience" be an illusion rather than an authentic encounter with God?

   _____
   _____
   _____
   _____
   _____
   _____

3. From John's narrative and the truths delineated on pages 78–81, can you express Christ's teaching regarding salvation and spiritual rebirth?

   _____
   _____
   _____
   _____
   _____
   _____

4. Can you personally express the reality of sorrow which results from chasing other "gods" in your life (Psalms 16:4)?

_____

_____

_____

_____

_____

_____

5. Now, take a moment and meditate upon what you possess in Jesus Christ. Are you able to list the blessings, the promises of joy?

_____

_____

_____

_____

_____

_____

6. Write out the first sentence of each of the three points which speak to deeper insight on God's "attachment of love" (p. 89, ff).

First: _____

_____

Second: _____

_____

Third: _____

_____

7. How do you explain God's love as a "wonderful antidote for fear"?

_____

_____

_____

_____

_____

_____

8. In Romans 8, the Apostle Paul discusses at length, the entourage of fear. As you list these, rehearse aloud Paul's punch line found in verse 35.

_____

_____

_____

_____

_____

_____

9. Provide the list of the only resources that God has given His troops to sustain them in this world (p. 94).

A. _____

B. _____

C. _____

D. _____

Notes

CHAPTER 7

Practicum

OK—it's your turn!

As you peruse the evaluation questions, remedial assignments, and rehab strategies, choose a particular area of your life where you are vulnerable to fear, anxiety, or chronic worry. Now, devise your own plan for troop preparedness using the practicum format of chapter 7. Discuss it with your study group, Christian leader, or Christian friend. Perfect your plan and begin putting it into action.

I. <u>Combat Arsenal—Battle-Ready Resources</u>

A. Presenting Issue:

_____

_____

_____

B. Reading Assignment:

_____

_____

_____

C. Remedial Prescription:

_____

_____

_____

II. Life Readiness—An Overarching Plan to Succeed

_____
_____
_____
_____
_____
_____
_____
_____
_____
_____
_____
_____
_____
_____
_____
_____
_____
_____
_____
_____
_____
_____
_____
_____
_____
_____
_____
_____
_____
_____
_____
_____
_____
_____
_____

Notes

ABOUT THE AUTHOR

Pastor Mark L. Graham has served the local church for nearly forty-five years. He has written extensively to provide biblical helps for those under his pastoral and counseling care. Founder of the Genesis Ministries, Inc. (www.genesisministry.org), and adjunct professor of biblical counseling for eight years with the Empire State Baptist Theological Seminary, Dr. Graham holds various degrees and diplomas in ministry, counseling and law. Currently, Pastor Graham lives with his wife, Diane, in Fayetteville, New York, where he counsels, writes, and scripts for his radio broadcast, Thinking Biblically, heard weekly over the Mars Hill Network.

The Grahams have four married children who serve Christ through the local church. They also enjoy their heritage of twelve grandchildren, two of whom live at home with Jesus.

Printed in the United States
by Baker & Taylor Publisher Services